A-HA!

The more you reflect,
The more you become!

Sorbojeet Chatterjee

ISBN
Paperback 979-8-89610-950-1
Hardcase 979-8-89673-825-1

THE 'UNBOOK' EXPERIENCE

If you are looking for jargon that you can brandish to appear intelligent, this book is not for you.

If your life is an eight-lane highway with no potholes or speed bumps, this book is not for you.

If you have it all figured out at work (and in life), this book is definitely not for you!

So, who is this book for?

Well, if you are a young professional or an emerging leader wishing to navigate the complexities of the workplace with little or no time (or inclination) to read, this book might just be what the doctor ordered.

My brave journey of attempting to craft an *'unbook'* experience began when I came across these vehement (and candid) views from casual readers for a design thinking project:

> *"Every personal development book should have just been a blog!"*

> *"Even if it is a book I like, I just can't read beyond the first 2 or 3 chapters!"*

> *"Most books are a case of information overdose, but I can't remember to implement anything."*

I wanted to design a book that is less about preaching and more about reflecting!

It sounds good on paper, but how does one go about implementing it? I found the answer in the process of coaching. Let's dive into this with a simple 2x2 matrix (often referred to as David Rock's TAPS model).

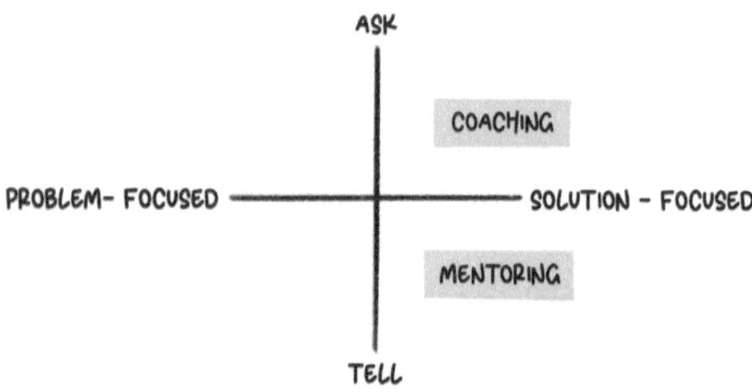

The 'Tell – Solution-focus' quadrant represents mentoring. A mentor shares their own rich experience and hence relies on a 'tell'-based approach. Most books would feature in this quadrant. The author is a subject matter expert, and all of us look forward to gaining from their experience and insights.

Coaching as a process falls in the 'Ask-Solution-focus' quadrant. A coach is not engaged for their subject matter expertise but for their ability to help unlock the coachee's potential.

Always remember, an effective coach has supreme belief in the coachee's ability to solve their own challenges.

Hence, I have mindfully discarded my author's hat where I 'tell' and instead put on my coach's hat and simply 'ask'. I have compiled some of the most powerful questions that have helped my coachees unlock their potential in the last few years. Moreover, I have complete faith in the notion that everyone has all the answers inside them. All I need to do is be a catalyst and trigger some powerful reflections.

The questions are organised across 14 themes that can be collectively described as workplace smarts. From 'being optimistic' to 'getting things done', every chapter will help you unlock new insights and bring your A-game to work.

Go ahead and think of this book as a personal coach in your pocket!

WAYS OF READING

The 'unbook' experience is not designed as a linear journey. Here are a few ways in which you can enjoy the book:

Disruptor
Did you ever play book cricket as a child? The same rules apply. Randomly open any page and reflect on a question.

Focused one
If there's a particular walk of your life that requires focus (like bouncing back after a failure or dealing with uncertainty), simply visit that chapter and reflect on all the questions.

Purist
You can always adopt the linear approach, starting with the first chapter and systematically working your way to the last one.

People's person
Another way to enjoy this book is to 'socialise' with it. Read it along with your friends, family, or colleagues and support each other in transforming insights into actions.

Regardless of your reading style, this book is designed to cater to everyone. Even if you are a reluctant reader, each chapter features a QR code that unlocks a video with the cheat code to ace each theme.

THANK YOU

Mrs. Doodle Monster (Sushmita Mukherjee) for bringing this book alive with her design and illustrations.

My colleague *Swapnil*, for helping me with the research and ensuring we meet every deadline, no matter how hard I tried to procrastinate!

Swetha, my publishing partner from Notion Press, for being a genuine friend and guide at every step.

Gitanjali Bagchi, my mother (and co-founder of our startup, Happ Coach), for a million things! Besides all the life lessons, she introduced me to copywriting and executive coaching. This book tries to be at the confluence of both these worlds.

Bani, my wife and pillar of strength, for patiently 'nudging' me to write a book over the past 10 years. Finally, I complied (like always!)

My daughter, *Anya*, for being my biggest cheerleader (and fiercest critic). This book is about reflecting, and nothing makes me reflect harder than trying to answer her questions!

WHAT LIES AHEAD

LET'S GET STARTED

Aryan had just taken over as the Commanding Officer of an army camp. During his evening walk, he saw 2 soldiers guarding a bench at the Central Park. It intrigued him.

The next day, while taking a walk, he saw that a couple of soldiers were guarding the bench once again. He walked up to them and bellowed, "Good evening! So, what treasure lies beneath that it takes my finest soldiers to guard it every day?"

"Sir! We don't know. We are just following the orders of the previous commander!"

Aryan thought it might be a long-standing tradition and didn't want to disrupt it immediately, but his curiosity lingered. He decided to call his predecessor.

"Well, my senior did it, and I didn't want to be the one to break the tradition. I am proud to say that I ensured we didn't miss a single day – come hail or sunshine!"

Aryan's curiosity compounded! He managed to trace a few of the former commanders and got the same reply. Finally, the rabbit hole led him to retired General Bakshi. Aryan was getting "curiouser and curiouser."

General Bakshi was now retired in a small town, spending his time tending to his kitchen garden.

"Sir, I am curious. What is so precious or sacred about the bench at Central Park? Two of my best soldiers have to guard it every day."

The general got visibly irritated. He thundered, "Why are those jokers still guarding it? Has the paint still not dried?"

Aren't some of us guilty of following instructions at the workplace without questioning their necessity or relevance? At times, we do it out of 'respect' for our manager, but more often, it's simply the convenient option. Either way, we seem to have forgotten the art of 'pause and reflect'.

Let's look at the primary objective of this book. Can you fill in the blanks:

Reading a book is just assimilating information unless you__________.

Failure teaches you nothing unless you __________.

Learning something new is a futile exercise unless you __________.

The past will keep repeating itself unless you __________.

Here the common answer is **Reflect!**

- *Reflect is the pause to think and assess options.*
- *Reflect is the nudge to get us started on the right path.*
- *Reflect is the bridge between feeling and effective action.*
- *Reflect is the sweet spot between the stimulus and the ideal response.*

In our busy lives, action (however mindless) is visible and hence rewarded. Reflection leads to superior outcomes but provides delayed gratification.

Hence, it is often neglected.

Always remember that autopilot is best restricted to aviation. The human brain is designed to think and reflect, not be in a state of continuous 'drift'.

Here is a quick and simplified explanation of how the brain works. The brain comprises 2 critical parts – let's call them the Feeler (Limbic System) and the Thinker (Prefrontal Cortex). As the name suggests, the 'Feeler' is the seat of emotion and is the dominant part of the brain. It controls our 'fight or flight' response. The 'Thinker' is the seat of intelligence and critical thinking.

The relationship between them is like a seesaw; if one is activated, it shuts down the other!

"Tell me what you're feeling?"

Isn't that the first question a coach, therapist, or even a friend would ask when they want to help? In simple terms, they are calming the feeler and activating the thinker by getting you to reflect.

This book is all about engaging your thinker through simple reflections. Answering these questions might not win you a million bucks in a television game show. They might even seem trivial at first glance. But when you spend a few moments reflecting, you will surely unlock some winning insights. It is bound to pay you back in spades!

GETTING THINGS DONE

Twenty pieces of uncooked spaghetti, one metre of string, one metre of masking tape, and one marshmallow!

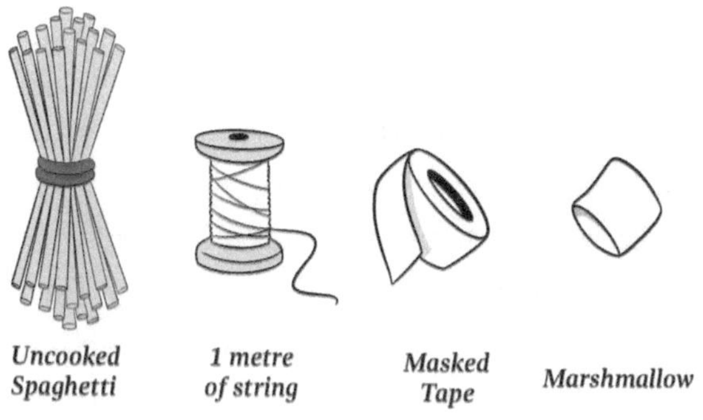

Uncooked Spaghetti

1 metre of string

Masked Tape

Marshmallow

The challenge is straightforward: work in a group to build a stable structure with the marshmallow on top. What is the tallest structure that you can build in just 18 minutes?

I first came across this design challenge (often referred to as The Spaghetti Tower) in a 2006 TED Talk by design consultant Peter Skillman. It has become my go-to activity to kickstart every design thinking workshop. I am fortunate enough to experience every action and emotion Skillman articulated in his speech.

Skillman worked with a diverse group comprising CEOs, MBA graduates, managers, and even kindergarten kids.

Can you guess which cohort performed the best and which group failed miserably?

Before I reveal that, let's understand the process followed by most groups. The team members would organise themselves, appoint a leader, discuss the tasks, spend a considerable amount of time debating ideas, and eventually select an approach through voting. Doesn't this feel eerily familiar to most meetings in the workplace?

In the pursuit of building consensus, most of the teams made little progress in building the spaghetti tower! In fact, one of the teams barely managed to put together a single version of the structure, and when it failed, there was no time for them to course-correct.

The worst-performing group was the MBA graduates. According to author Daniel Coyle in his book *The Culture Code*, *"The business school students appear to be collaborating, but in fact, they are engaged in a process psychologists call status management. They are figuring out where they fit into the larger picture: Who is in charge?"*

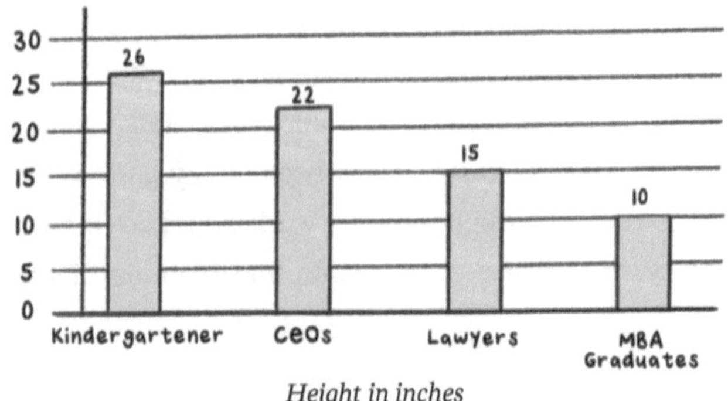

Height in inches

Surprisingly, the group of kindergarten students performed the best. Now, how could a bunch of kids outperform business leaders and management graduates from premier institutions?

Skillman said, "*The kindergarteners didn't spend 15 minutes deciding who is going to be CEO of Spaghetti Corporation. They immediately began building and learning.*" The 'inexperienced' children collaborated without any ego and kept iterating.

Essentially, they didn't form committees, indulge in endless meetings, or blame each other if something didn't work out. They kept at it until the task was completed.

In the modern workplace, where uncertainty and complexity can't be escaped, single-minded focus and the hustle to get the job done are superpowers. We are surrounded by people who think, plan, talk, and even begin the task. But the real champion is the one who gets things done!

Scan the QR code to unlock the best practices to get things done.

Do you get distracted easily? Can you identify 3 things you can do to build focus and become distraction-proof?

Distractions lead to missed goals, resulting in guilt, unhappiness and a vicious cycle of low productivity.

Can you identify 5 tech products that can significantly enhance your productivity?

____

____

____

____

____

Technology can improve efficiency by speeding up processes and reducing errors in repetitive and mundane tasks.

On a scale of 1 to 10, how would you rate your ability to delegate? Can you identify 3 tasks that you can start delegating?

____

____

____

____

____

Delegation, when done well, creates valuable time, strengthens team capabilities, and fosters a culture of trust and accountability.

Are you a successful multitasker? Can you try to identify 3 harmful effects of multitasking?

____

____

____

____

____

A-ha!

Multitasking may seem productive, but in reality, it slows us down. The human brain can't cope with rapidly switching between tasks, making us less productive in the long run.

Do you suffer from the 'disease to please'? Can you think of 3 instances where you should have politely refused but ended up saying yes?

____

____

____

____

____

Saying 'yes' too often can be detrimental as you may unknowingly take on more tasks than you can complete.

What was the last pointless and long meeting that you attended? Can you identify 3 things you can do to ensure meetings are structured and outcome-focused?

____

____

____

____

____

Research shows that approximately 31 hours are wasted each month in pointless meetings. Beyond wasting collective time, these meetings can leave attendees feeling disengaged, especially when there's no clear takeaway.

Do you feel stressed and anxious as your to-do list keeps growing? Can you identify 5 things you can do to keep your stress levels in check?

____

____

____

____

____

Stress is inversely proportional to productivity and directly proportional to worry and time-wasting.

Can you identify 5 'time wasters' in your regular day that inadvertently take up a lot more time than you bargained for?

____

____

____

____

____

'Time-wasting' activities are a source of frustration for all of us. They creep in subconsciously, stealing precious time. Becoming mindful is the first step towards eliminating them.

Are you a perennial procrastinator? Can you think of a task that you keep putting off without any reason? Can you identify 3 things you can do to complete that task without further procrastination?

____

____

____

____

____

Procrastination can lead to missed deadlines and a backlog of unfinished tasks. Moreover, it creates a last-minute rush to complete work, resulting in low-quality output and increased stress.

Being a perfectionist is a wonderful thing. But can you identify 3 instances where, in order to achieve perfection, you spent much more time than required, thus hampering your productivity?

____

____

____

____

____

Don't let perfectionism become the enemy of productivity. Spending too much time to achieve the perfect output for an unimportant task can leave you with little time for important tasks.

TAKING A CALL

24 November 1993: India and South Africa were battling it out in the low-scoring semi-finals of the Hero Cup. India had scored a modest 195, and the Proteas were cruising to victory. They needed just 6 runs to win in the final over, and 'strongman' Brian McMillan was batting on 46 runs. It seemed like a done deal! It wouldn't take more than 1 or 2 hits for South Africa to make it to the finals and for McMillan to score a well-deserved half-century.

The Indian captain, Azharuddin, had a decision to make – who would bowl the last over? India's strike bowler, Srinath, had 2 overs left; the experienced Kapil Dev had 2 overs as well, while the all-rounder Salil Ankola had 4 overs left. If you were the captain, who would you turn to?

Azharuddin had only seconds to assess it all—the form and skill of each bowler, the behaviour of the pitch, the vulnerabilities of the batsmen—every detail critical to making an informed decision on the spot.

He must have realised that the 2 most successful bowlers for India were Anil Kumble (2 for 29 runs) and part-timer Ajay Jadeja (2 for 31 runs). I guess the slower bowlers got more purchase of the wicket, which had been worn out by the end of the day.

He went ahead with a bold choice. He picked Sachin Tendulkar to bowl the final over! It was the first over Sachin would bowl in the match. I am sure several factors would have contributed to Azhar's decision, like Tendulkar's tactical shrewdness, bowling style, confidence level, and his ability to take ownership.

Well, we know how the game panned out. Tendulkar gave away just 3 runs, and India proudly marched ahead to the finals.

I often wonder – was the captain hailed a genius because the outcome of his decision was favourable? Would he have been labelled a fool if McMillan hit a 6 off the first ball and won the match?

One can't escape making decisions. Every day begins with a decision – an indulgent breakfast with waffles and pancakes or a healthier alternative like oats! Similarly, it ends with a decision too – Binge-watch your favourite series on Netflix or read a book before retiring. Life is a series of decisions in varying shapes and sizes!

Have you realised the word decide has the same suffix as homicide, suicide, and genocide? The suffix 'cide' comes from Latin and means to kill or strike down. Sounds scary?

You might wonder what killing has to do with decision-making. Well, to decide simply means to kill options.

At the workplace, most decisions have a cascading and long-term impact, such as deciding which candidate to hire or which new product to launch. In fact, in several instances, one may not have access to all the facts and data points but is still expected to make an 'informed' decision.

Ironically, not making a decision is also a decision.

Scan the QR code to master an effective decision-making framework

Can you think of a personal or professional decision where you spent a lot of time and effort researching all the information? Can you identify 3 best practices required to diligently research every aspect before making a decision?

____

____

____

____

Thorouyh research plays a critical role in evaluating all options and helps make a well-informed decision.

Can you identify an area where you need to make a decision in the near future? What are the top 3 options that come into your mind? Now, can you think harder and come up with 3 more alternatives?

____

____

____

____

____

Identifying alternatives is one of the most critical steps in decision-making. You must go beyond the initial few options.

Can you identify 3 biases that you fall prey to while making decisions? How can you eliminate these biases going forward?

____

____

____

____

____

Multiple biases may play a role in influencing your decisions. Being aware and acknowledging their existence is the first step towards being mindful and eliminating these biases.

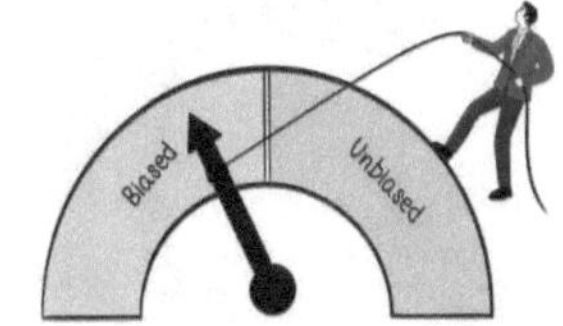

Can you think of a major decision that you had to make recently where the outcome was irreversible? Identify 3 things you would do differently for an irreversible decision compared to a reversible one.

____

____

____

____

____

Irreversible decisions might require us to slow down and ensure we consider all the available information and evaluate the pros and cons of all the options.

When was the last time you sought advice or perspectives from others (friends, family, colleagues) while making an important decision? Can you identify 3 benefits of listening to multiple voices in decision-making?

____

____

____

____

____

The process of collaborative decision-making looks at multiple points of view and helps eliminate individual biases while expanding the option pool.

Do you maintain a decision journal? Can you think of the last major decision that you had to make and note down the challenges, alternatives, reason for finalising the decision, and the expected outcome?

____

____

____

____

____

Nobel Laureate Daniel Kahneman suggests that the best way to test the quality of your decisions is to maintain a decision journal and revisit the reasoning and expected outcome.

Emotional outbursts can often derail the most critical decisions. Can you remember an instance where an emotional outburst derailed an outcome?

It is human for emotions to affect decision-making. However, being able to keep our emotions in check helps us avoid impulsive choices and make rational decisions.

How often do you evaluate the outcome of your decisions? Can you identify one decision that didn't yield the desired results? If you could go back in time, what would you do differently if you had to tackle the same challenge again?

____

____

____

____

____

Committing to a decision is not the final step in decision-making. It is critical to evaluate your decision, monitor your decision, and course-correct wherever possible.

Can you recollect a decision where the outcome could have been favourable if you had reached out to an expert or mentor for insights? Can you identify 3 benefits of reaching out to experts in case you are feeling stuck?

____

____

____

____

____

When you feel stuck or there is not enough data to make an informed decision, relying on an expert might increase the probability of success.

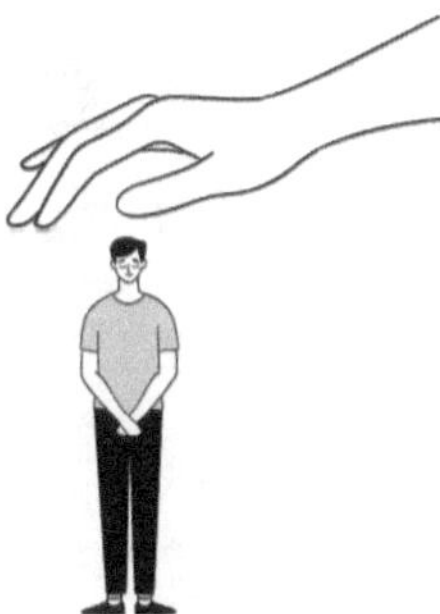

Do you feel there is any merit in relying on instincts while making decisions? Can you recollect a few decisions where you went with your instincts? How comfortable were you?

____

____

____

____

____

We don't live in a utopian world where we have access to all the information. You must be prepared to rely on your instincts to make a quick decision.

PRACTISING COMPASSION

"One chicken burger and a pint of beer, please!" You walk into a restaurant famished and order what you think will be served in no time.

It takes longer than expected, and you're served grilled fish and a tall glass of chocolate milkshake. I bet you'd be angry—or maybe even hangry! How could they mess it up so badly?

Would you care to visit a restaurant chain that gets 37% of its orders wrong? And yet, 99% of their customers are happy. If you hear a loud burst of laughter, it simply means that yet another table was served the wrong order.

Welcome to the Restaurant of Mistaken Orders in Tokyo!

This unique pop-up concept, which originated in Japan in 2017, employs servers who have dementia, meaning there's a high chance that your order might get mixed up. The restaurant's mission is to provide the elderly with a sense of purpose while debunking common myths about dementia

The gentle surprise of inadvertent human mistakes has, in a way, become the true product of the restaurant—more so than the meal itself. Much of the laughter that fills the eatery comes from the pleasant surprise of being unexpectedly served something different.

I am sure if you visited this restaurant, you would demonstrate the same degree of compassion as everyone else. But would you extend that same compassion to a team member who makes a glaring error during a high-stakes meeting?

In this restaurant, the challenges faced by the servers were visible and clearly conveyed, making it easier to demonstrate compassion. However, we might not always fathom what a colleague or a stranger is going through. So, how do we continue to show compassion in such cases?

It's simple: always give the benefit of doubt!

Compassion can be the magic pill that lights up even the most anxious of moments. In fact, a Johns Hopkins study found that just 40 seconds of compassion can significantly lower another person's anxiety. Beyond improving employee

engagement and morale, a compassionate workforce is more productive, retains talent better, and significantly reduces burnout.

Organisations often spend endless hours in boardroom discussions to foster a culture of diversity and inclusion. Creating a mindset of compassion might be the perfect first step.

Scan the QR code to unlock the best practices to build your compassion quotient.

Do you listen to truly understand, or do you listen merely to respond? Can you identify 5 things you can actively listen for to pick up cues and unstated issues?

____

____

____

____

____

Active listening builds deep connections and helps colleagues understand and appreciate each other's perspectives.

When was the last time you reached out to a colleague or a team member just to check on their well-being? Can you identify 3 benefits of such check-ins?

____

____

____

____

____

Proactively checking in on your team members and offering ideas and solutions helps create a culture of trust and camaraderie.

When was the last time you stepped in for a colleague who was going through a personal challenge? How did they feel? More importantly, how did you feel?

____

____

____

____

____

Being mindful of a colleague facing personal challenges and stepping in to assist can make them feel supported and secure at work.

Can you recall a time when you collaborated with colleagues who had opinions different from yours? Identify 3 actions you can take to avoid judgement and demonstrate compassion.

____

____

____

____

____

Embracing differences in people without judging them fosters a more connected team and workplace.

Can you remember a time when your manager or colleague encouraged you before a critical task? How did it make you feel? Can you think of 3 ways you can regularly offer words of encouragement to your team and colleagues?

____

____

____

____

____

Offering words of encouragement before important tasks or deadlines helps reassure colleagues when they feel uncertain.

Do you tend to be tougher on yourself than on others? Can you identify 3 ways you can practise more self-compassion?

____

____

____

____

____

When you are kinder to yourself, you become more resilient and productive.

If someone at work seems out of sorts and is making more mistakes than usual, how can you show compassion towards them? Can you think of 3 benefits of adopting a compassionate approach?

____

____

____

____

____

A simple act of compassion when someone is having a tough day fosters a sense of belonging and creates deeper connections.

Can you recall a time when someone extended an act of kindness, however small, when you least expected it? How did it make you feel? Can you identify 5 people to whom you would like to offer a random act of kindness over the next few days?

____

____

____

____

Kindness never goes out of fashion! Random acts of kindness build strong bonds and contribute to a more compassionate world.

Think of a time when a team member or a colleague faced a setback and didn't achieve the desired outcome. How did you react to it? Can you identify 3 ways in which you could have shown more compassion?

____

____

____

____

____

While celebrating wins is important, it's equally critical to take a compassionate approach after failures to lift the morale of the team and create a positive work environment.

On a scale of 1 to 10 (low to high), how diverse is your team? Can you identify 5 ways you can make your team more inclusive?

____

____

____

____

Compassion is key to building inclusive workplaces. An inclusive culture attracts better talent and enhances creativity.

BEING OPTIMISTIC

Jonathan called his father and said, "I need a loan. Am I just dreaming? Should I just come back to Chicago?"

Leonard pacified his son and said, "I'll give you the loan; you gotta stay put."

He ended the call by saying something that stayed with Jonathan and became a part of rock 'n' roll history!

Here is some context – Jonathan was a struggling musician who had left his home in Chicago and was trying to make a mark in LA. Despite his hard efforts, nothing seemed to be going right.

The final straw came when his pet dog was hit by a car, and he didn't have enough money to cover the $900 vet bill. Struggling to pay his rent as it was, his only option was to call his father for help.

A few months after the phone call, Jonathan Cain was invited to join the band 'Journey' as a keyboardist, where he co-wrote his first song.

The song became a monster hit and continues to be one of the most streamed songs. Can you guess the song?

The song title was borrowed from the parting words his dad told him during the phone call, 'Don't stop believin'.

- *If you are a sales professional and the current quarter doesn't look so good,*
- *If you are a team lead and someone in your team is not powering through.*
- *If you are a first-time founder and product-market fit continues to elude you.*

Leonard Friga's advice will always serve you well - Don't stop believin'.

As per a study by Leadership IP, which surveyed over 11,000 employees, maintaining an optimistic outlook can significantly boost engagement and productivity at work. In fact, the benefits of optimism can surpass even those of having a great manager!

In a world filled with peddlers of doom and gloom, a 'sunshine take' on everything from work to life is often all it takes to power through.

Like they say, *"Pessimists are usually right, but optimists change the world!"*

Scan the QR code to unlock the secret sauce and focus on the opportunity in every difficulty, not the other way around.

When facing a problem, are you someone who focuses on the problem or the solution? Can you identify 3 things you can do to become more solution-focused?

____

____

____

____

____

Focusing on solutions instead of problems helps you see the possibilities rather than the limitations.

Think of the 5 most optimistic people in your social circle (friends, family, colleagues, etc.). Can you identify a few of their strengths that you can borrow to increase your optimism quotient?

____

____

____

____

____

Positivity begets more positivity! Positive people are a source of motivation and inspiration to stay on track.

Have you tried visualising success in the midst of a challenge? What could be the possible benefits of positive visualisation?

____

____

____

____

____

Positive visualisation can help you stay motivated and focused on your goals.

How do you handle negative thoughts during a tough situation? Can you think of 3 ways to deal with negative emotions effectively?

____

____

____

____

____

Optimism is not the lack of negative thoughts. The awareness of them helps resolve it in your head.

Have you tried journaling your thoughts and feelings? Can you think of a few ways journaling can help you while facing a challenging situation?

____

____

____

____

____

Journaling helps you become more self-aware and helps in resolving negative thoughts and emotions. Additionally, it serves to anchor positive emotions.

If you had to send a thank you note to 3 people right now, who would they be, and what would you thank them for?

____

____

____

____

____

Gratitude is a gift that keeps giving. In positive psychology, gratitude helps relish good experiences, deal with adversity, and stay optimistic.

Do you spend a lot of your time thinking about the uncontrollable in a situation? Can you identify 3 controllables you can start focusing on in a challenging situation?

____

____

____

____

____

Focusing on the controllable won't make the challenge disappear. However, it will help you stay positive and eliminate unnecessary stress.

In the midst of a tough situation, are you hard on yourself, or do you tend to demonstrate self-compassion? Can you think of 3 things you can do to show more self-compassion?

____

____

____

____

____

Studies show that people who practice self-compassion are less likely to experience stress and depression and more likely to be optimistic about the future.

Are you able to smile even in the midst of chaos and crisis? Can you think of 3 things that make you smile?

____

____

____

____

____

Research shows that smiling releases endorphins, making it a powerful way to relieve stress and maintain a positive outlook.

Is there a go-to quote or slogan that you keep repeating to stay positive? Can you think of 3 phrases that can help you stay optimistic?

____

____

____

____

____

"You've got this!" Believing in your abilities and trusting yourself is the foundation of staying optimistic.

EMBRACING UNCERTAINTY

The University College London performed a novel experiment to measure the impact of uncertainty.

Students were split into 2 groups. The 1st group had a 90% probability of getting an electric shock, while the 2nd group had a 50% probability. The stress levels of both groups were monitored.

Can you guess which group had higher stress levels?

Most of us would be tempted to point towards the 1st group. They were almost certain that they would get an electric shock.

Would you believe that while the chances of getting an electric shock for the 2nd group were significantly lower, their stress level was 3 times higher? Sounds unbelievable?

Well, that is how uncertainty creates undue stress.

As per research by EY, 50% of CEOs named 'uncertainty' as the single greatest external threat to their businesses.

Let me take you back on a ride in a time machine. Assume it is the beginning of 2010, and you have been assigned to lead a project to reimagine the future in 2020. You kickstart the programme with a senior management brainstorming session in Bali.

Over the next few years, several offsites take place across exotic locations around the world. Odds-on favourite, most challenges would be around staying relevant for millennials & Gen Zs, accelerating the pace of digitisation, or being sustainable and environmentally friendly.

In fact, most organisations would have participated in a similar exercise. Do you think any group would have predicted that a strain of virus would hold the entire world hostage and sustained lockdowns would be imposed in most countries? A single uncertain event negatively impacted the global GDP with a 7-8% degrowth.

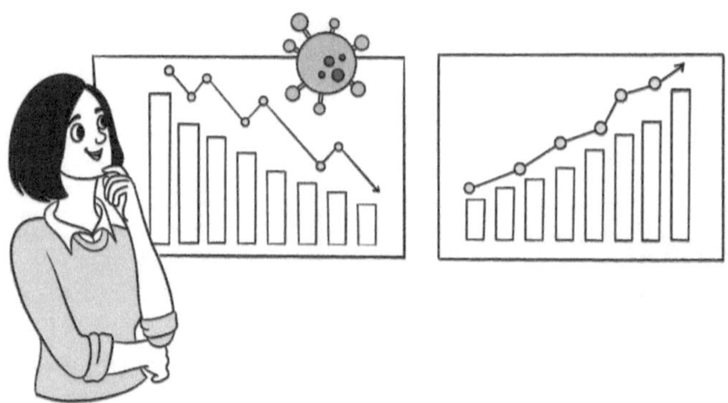

But digital adoption accelerated due to the COVID-19 pandemic. It is often said that the rate of growth in a few weeks surpassed the growth in a decade!

The COVID era, like every other high-uncertainty event, split the world into 'haves' and 'have nots'. Success will always reward those who 'have' the ability to navigate uncertainty and power through in spite of all odds.

And this is certainly not the last we have seen of uncertainty!

Scan the QR code to master embracing uncertainty.

What is the most important project you are currently working on? Can you articulate your desirable outcome? Assume that your action plan is getting derailed. Can you think of a Plan B?

____

____

____

____

____

Contingency planning allows you to minimise risks and the impact of uncertainties in business operations.

Think of an uncertainty that is bothering you at work. Can you identify any 5 people you can collaborate with to help navigate the situation?

____

____

____

____

____

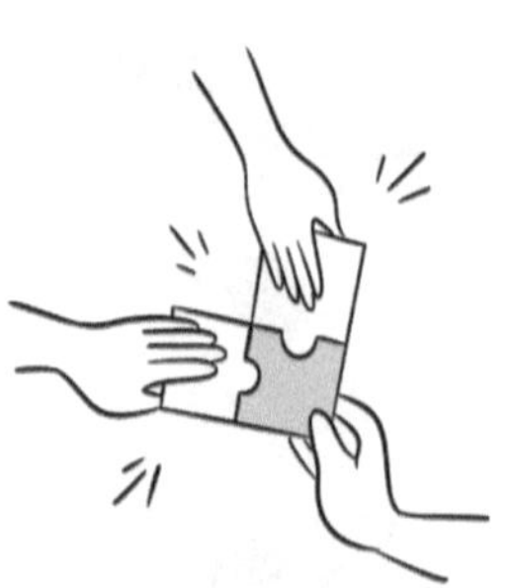

Collaboration brings together diverse perspectives, enabling teams to tackle uncertainty with greater clarity and innovation in the workplace.

What is your communication style when faced with uncertainty? Identify 3 things you can do to be more transparent in your communication.

____

____

____

____

____

Transparent communication dispels doubts and rumours, providing a realistic understanding of the uncertainties and the challenges they pose.

What is your relationship with uncertainty? Can you identify 5 strategies to stay calm the next time you encounter uncertainty?

____

____

____

____

____

Staying calm under pressure sharpens our clarity and empowers us to make more thoughtful, effective decisions.

Think of an uncertain situation at work. Can you identify 3 things that are controllable (by you) and 3 things that are uncontrollable?

____

____

____

____

____

By focusing on what you can control, you will not feel as overwhelmed during uncertain times.

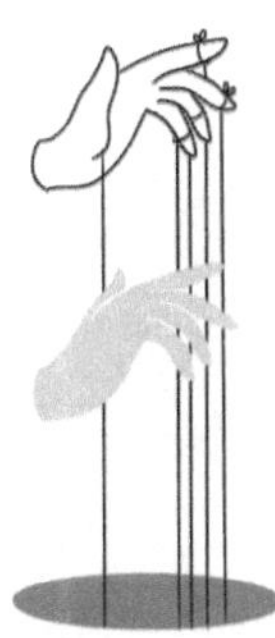

During uncertain times, what occupies more mind space - worrying about what can happen or focusing on what you can do? Can you identify 3 things you can mindfully do to focus on 'What Is' and not 'What If'?

____

____

____

____

____

When encountering uncertainty, we tend to fall into the web of thought distortions and distract our minds with negative thoughts. Concentrating on the present can help us stay calm and focus better.

On a scale of 1-10, how flexible are you in adapting to change? Can you identify 3 things that you can do to become more agile and flexible?

____

____

____

____

____

Agility is the must-have asset required to master change and manage risk. After all, today's problems can't be solved with yesterday's solutions!

Think of the toughest challenge you are facing in terms of uncertainty. Can you identify 5 opportunities that this challenge can unlock?

____

____

____

____

____

We all have a natural tendency towards negativity bias. However, by consciously reframing challenges as opportunities, we can shift our perspective and begin focusing on the positive side of things.

Can you identify 3 areas where you are in cruise control? What can you proactively do to challenge yourself and step out of your comfort zone?

____

____

____

____

____

Challenging yourself and moving out of your comfort zone can make you comfortable with increased levels of uncertainty.

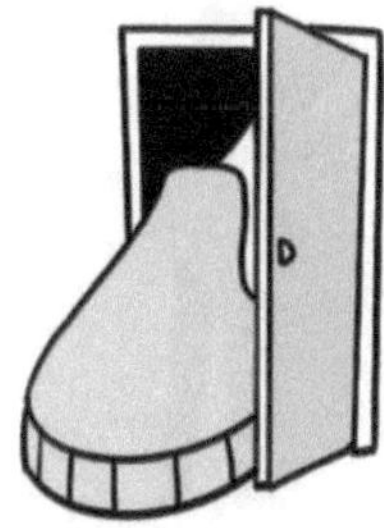

Identify an uncertain situation that you navigated successfully. Can you articulate 3 action points that helped you emerge victorious?

____

____

____

____

____

Reflecting on past success provides a strong foundation to plan for the future with confidence. You have done it before; there is no reason you can't do it again.

BOOSTING CONFIDENCE

18 July 1980: India built an experimental Satellite Launch Vehicle (SLV-3) and successfully launched the Rohini Satellite into orbit. ISRO's 48-year-old Project Director was beaming from ear to ear as he narrated the success stories on behalf of his team in the press conference.

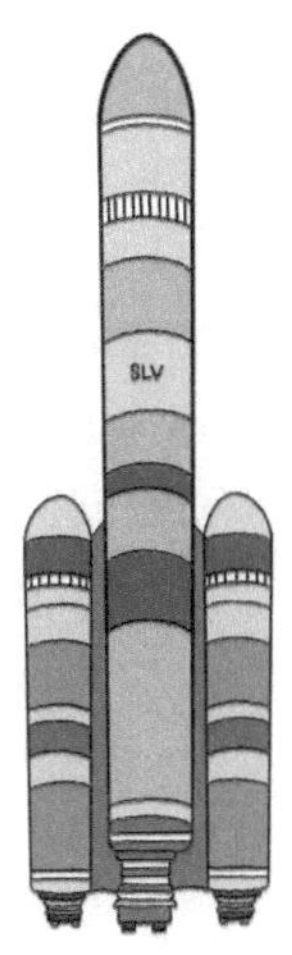

And why not? India had finally become part of the exclusive space club of countries that could indigenously develop the technology needed to launch satellites.

All the enthusiasm and euphoria was a welcome departure from the grief and dejection faced by the team a year back.

In July 1979, the first attempt at this mission failed due to a faulty valve. Instead of making it to the history books, it ended up in the Bay of Bengal. Understandably, the Project Director was devastated by the failure and apprehensive about facing tough questions from a hostile press. The project cost over Rs 20 Crores. As per the prevailing dollar rate in 1979, it works out to USD 25 million. I am sure the angry press was eager to assign blame.

However, Satish Dhawan, the then Chairman of ISRO, decided to address the press conference. He took ownership of the failure and made it a point to emphasise his continued confidence in the same team.

Dhawan's confidence in the team paid off in spades! The outcome was a spectacular return, validating both the taxpayers' investment and his unwavering belief in the team.

The Project Director recounted this story multiple times and always acknowledged that, "the Chairman had more confidence in me than I had in myself."

In case you are curious, the Project Director of the SLV-3 was none other than the former President of India, Dr. APJ Abdul Kalam.

I have a similar story from my formative years at work. I was a management trainee, and in my enthusiasm to release my first print ad, I took a shortcut in the quality check process. As a result, a typo slipped through my 'watchful' eyes. I remember asking my manager if he was going to fire me.

And he calmly replied, "I have just spent a lot of money

on your education. How can I let you go?"

That booster shot of confidence helped me power through several ups and downs at work and in life. I still don't know if I was able to pay him back for his grace and generosity, but I have mindfully tried to pay it forward by showing faith in all my team members, especially when the chips are down.

Demonstrating confidence and providing frequent validation doesn't cost anything and is often the secret sauce that flips every doubtful 'Can I?' to a confident 'I can!'

Scan the QR code to unlock the best practices to build confidence.

Do you celebrate the little victories? Can you think of 3 such wins from the past 2 weeks that truly deserved a moment of recognition?

____

____

____

____

____

Celebrating small wins fuels your motivation and lifts your confidence, empowering you to keep moving forward.

Can you identify your top 5 strengths at work? Reflect on a few instances of success where you harnessed these strengths. How did you feel?

____

____

____

____

____

Cultivating a positive mindset by emphasising your strengths rather than dwelling on weaknesses can significantly boost confidence.

Identify a goal you want to achieve. Now, assume you've achieved it and visualise, in granular detail, the day it happens. What are you wearing? How do you feel? How are your friends and colleagues congratulating you? Visualise the step-by-step process you followed to get there.

____

____

____

____

____

Visualising your success builds both confidence and self-belief. By envisioning your achievements, you're practising success itself, setting the stage for it to become a reality.

Try observing yourself in the mirror and identify 3 things you can do to make your body language stronger.

____

____

____

____

____

A confident body language can elevate your self-esteem and empower you to feel your best.

Are you fully prepared for each presentation, or do you prefer to wing it? Can you identify 3 things you can do to ensure you're thoroughly prepared for your next presentation or meeting?

____

____

____

____

____

Being well-prepared boosts your confidence as the risk of uncertainty is largely mitigated.

Can you identify 3 things you can start doing to communicate more assertively?

____

____

____

____

____

Speaking assertively allows you to communicate more effectively, set boundaries, and build confidence.

Can you think of an area where you want to improve? Identify 3 people you trust who can give you honest and relevant feedback. When will you reach out to them for feedback?

____

____

____

____

____

Seeking constructive feedback fuels growth, sharpens self-awareness, builds resilience, and strengthens relationships.

Can you identify 5 confident people (friends, family members, colleagues, etc) you like to spend time with? How can you imbibe some of their confidence?

____

____

____

____

____

Positive people serve as a source of inspiration and motivation. They help you become confident and stay focused on your goals.

Do you like to invest time and effort in learning new things? Identify 3 new things you have learned in the last 3 months. How are you implementing what you've learned?

____

____

____

____

____

Continuous learning and self-improvement are key to building confidence.

It is human nature to compare yourself with others, but one should ideally focus on one's own journey. Can you identify 3 areas where your current self has significantly improved?

____

____

____

____

Comparing yourself to others can be harmful and lead to a lack of self-worth, undermining your confidence.

MANAGING STRESS

Stress is the new pandemic; it just hasn't been declared yet.

As an executive coach, I work with professionals from all walks of life. Most young professionals in their 30s are ambitious and want to achieve breakthrough success. They acknowledge that stress is a byproduct of corporate success and are willing to pay the 'small price'. It doesn't deter them in the least.

Ironically, senior professionals in their 40s and 50s feel the stress was just not worth it and rue the harmful effects of it on their health and relationships. They are willing to trade some of the material success for peace and balance.

I often feel tempted to get these cohorts to talk to each other.

Stress is rightly called the silent killer. It kills your dreams, motivation, confidence, relationships, and much more. Often, by the time you realise it, the damage is irreversible.

Stress is the leading cause of 60% of all human illnesses and diseases. In fact, it accounts for 3 out of 4 doctor's visits. According to the American Psychological Association, chronic stress is linked to the 6 leading causes of death: heart disease, cancer, lung ailments, accidents, cirrhosis of the liver, and suicide. It is, indeed, a silent killer!

Let's examine some findings on mental wellness

from the India Wellness Index 2024 by ICICI Lombard. Factors contributing to mental wellness include workplace pressure, lack of adequate mental health support, and challenges with work-life balance.

In 2024, mental wellness declined for the 3rd consecutive year, reflecting rising levels of stress and anxiety.

- Millennials and Gen Zs saw the highest decline.
- The mental wellness score among corporate employees is 13% lower than the overall score.
- 80% of respondents faced at least one symptom of stress.
- 33% of respondents reported high levels of 'daily' stress.

The World Health Organisation (WHO) reports that stress-related illnesses are estimated to cost the world economy approximately $1 trillion in lost productivity annually, and the damage extends beyond the workplace.

Here are a few insights from global research conducted by the UKG Workforce Institute:

- *60% of employees say their job impacts their mental health more than anything else.*
- *Work stress negatively affects employees' home life (71%), well-being (64%), and relationships (62%).*
- *40% of the C-suite say they will likely quit within a year due to work-related stress.*

The tragic story of 26-year-old Anna Sebastian Perayil should never be forgotten. She joined a 'Big 4' audit firm and tragically lost her life to work-related stress.

Anna's mother penned a heartfelt letter to the CEO of the firm. She wrote – *"Anna was always a fighter, from childhood through her academic years, where she excelled in everything she did. She was a school topper and a college topper, excelled in extracurricular activities, and passed her CA exams with distinction. She worked tirelessly, giving her all to meet the demands placed on her. However, the workload, new environment, and long hours took a toll on her physically, emotionally, and mentally. She began experiencing anxiety, sleeplessness, and stress soon after joining, but she kept pushing herself, believing that hard work and perseverance were the keys to success."*

She further added, *"This is a systemic issue that goes beyond individual managers or teams. The relentless demands and the pressure to meet unrealistic expectations are not sustainable, and they cost us the life of a young woman with so much potential."*

We all grew up hearing—and perhaps internalising—the adage, "Hard work never killed anyone." It is bunkum! When hard work tips over to overwork and creates high stress, it can be fatal. And don't let anyone else determine your level of stress—not your manager or your family members. Everyone's ability to cope with stress is different, and you are the only voice that matters.

While Anna's story created quite a brouhaha on social media for a few days, it faded quickly, and all of us were back to mindlessly climbing the corporate ladder and leading our stressful lives. And while the young girl's story might have been forgotten, we should never forget-*Stress is a silent killer!*

Scan the QR code to unlock the best practices to manage stress

Do you find it easy to say 'No' to people, or do you suffer from the 'disease to please'? Can you identify 5 things you can do, set clear boundaries and say 'No' when necessary for your well-being?

Setting boundaries is crucial in managing stress. It allows you to focus on what is important.

When was the last time you took a break from work? Was it truly a break, or were you still plugged in? Can you think of 3 ways to ensure you take a complete break from work?

____

____

____

____

____

Taking a break helps you to reduce stress and feel more rested, productive, and focused when you return to work.

On a scale of 1 to 10, how would you rate your delegation skills? Can you identify 5 tasks or activities that you can start delegating from today?

____

____

____

____

____

Delegation can help reduce stress by allowing you to focus on your core competencies and priorities while empowering your team members.

Do you tend to set unrealistic and overly ambitious goals in a quest to overachieve? Identify 3 things you can do to make your goals more realistic.

____

____

____

____

____

Setting realistic goals increases the probability of success, boosting overall positivity and confidence, thereby reducing stress.

What is your favourite hobby? When was the last time you spent more than an hour on it? Can you think of 3 ways to actively dedicate more time to your hobby?

____

____

____

____

____

According to research, people who pursue active hobbies are less likely to suffer from stress and depression.

Can you name your 5 closest friends? How much time have you spent with them in the last few weeks? Can you identify 3 ways to increase the frequency of catching up with your friends?

____

____

____

____

____

Spending time with friends increases your sense of belonging, boosts happiness, and reduces stress.

Do you have a coach or mentor you can open up to when feeling stressed? Can you identify 5 benefits of having a trusted coach or mentor for stress management?

____

____

____

____

____

Working with a coach or mentor can help you manage stress by providing support, guidance, and a safe space to share your concerns.

We all feel overwhelmed at times. Can you identify 3 benefits of breaking challenges into smaller tasks and prioritising them?

____

____

____

____

____

Prioritising tasks can reduce stress and improve productivity by helping you focus on what's important.

Have you tried any mindfulness exercises when stress dominates your mindspace? Can you think of 3 benefits of practising deep breathing exercises when feeling stressed?

____

____

____

____

____

Mindfulness helps you stay in the present moment and avoid being overwhelmed or reacting to stressful situations.

How often do you exercise in a week? How do you feel after a session of any physical activity, such as playing a sport, working out in the gym, or even a simple walk?

____

____

____

____

____

Physical activity, such as a brisk walk, helps reduce stress by lowering cortisol (the stress hormone) levels.

BOUNCING BACK

This teenager made a blistering start, scoring an impressive 98 points with her first 10 shots at the women's 10-metre air pistol event at the Tokyo Olympics. *And then, tragedy struck.*

The 19-year-old's pistol malfunctioned. The lever in the pistol was broken and was preventing the barrel from functioning smoothly.

As per the rules, the jury allowed the defective part to be replaced and not the entire gun. In spite of losing precious minutes, she didn't give up and came back to complete what she had started. However, her grit wasn't enough to compensate for the lost time and opportunity. She missed qualifying for the finals by a mere 2 points!

The heartbreak led the young girl to contemplate quitting the sport. She didn't even look at her gun or practise for quite a few days.

According to an article in *The Indian Express*, her moment of epiphany came when she was holidaying with her family in Kerala. She suddenly found herself holding a kettle filled with hot water and pointing it at a wall, almost simulating the arm stability exercise.

And she knew what she had to do next.

She said to herself, 'I am getting restless; I really need to get back.'

Her pistol may have malfunctioned, but her mindset didn't!

And what a comeback it was. Manu Bhaker, fuelled by unwavering determination, won 2 bronze medals and secured an impressive 4th place in a third event at the next Olympics in Paris.

Manu Bhaker became the first Indian athlete to win 2 medals in the same edition of the Olympics. In fact, she almost won 3 medals. And I am sure the near miss in the women's 25-metre air pistol event is just the fuel she needs to come back even stronger in the next Olympics!

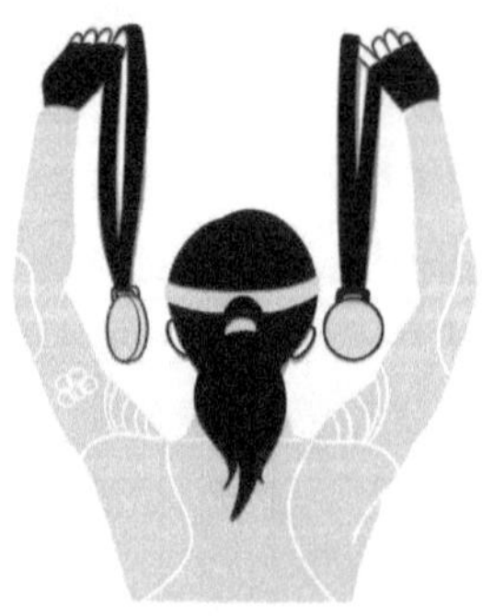

Inspirational stories of resilience in reel or real life have one common theme: the hero's journey- *the turnaround from setback to bounce back.* After all, enthusiasm is common, but resilience is rare.

Now, here is a popular storytelling framework used by Pixar in most of its blockbuster movies:

Once upon a time, there was a _______________________.

Every day, _______________________.

One day _______________________.

Because of that, _______________________.

Until finally _______________________.

Go ahead and fill in the blanks to create your blockbuster story of resilience and bounce back.

Scan the QR code to unlock the best practices to build the 'bouncing back' muscle.

On a scale of 1 to 10, how would you rate your resilience level? Can you identify 3 things you can do to increase your resilience?

____

____

____

____

____

Resilience is like shock absorbers that can help you cope with challenges and handle adversity. Thus, the higher your resilience quotient, the greater your ability to bounce back!

Are you hard on yourself if you don't achieve the desired goal? Can you think of a few things you can start doing to demonstrate self-compassion?

Being kind to yourself helps build confidence, remain positive, and stay motivated. Thus, making it easier to bounce back from setbacks.

Can you recall an incident where you gave up at the first sign of a challenge? Identify 3 things that you could do to stay persistent?

____

____

____

____

____

Persistence is the ability to remain goal-focused even in the midst of challenges and obstacles. It paves the way for a comeback after every setback!

When was the last time you felt devastated by a failure? Can you identify 3 things you learned from that incident that will serve you well in the future?

____

____

____

____

____

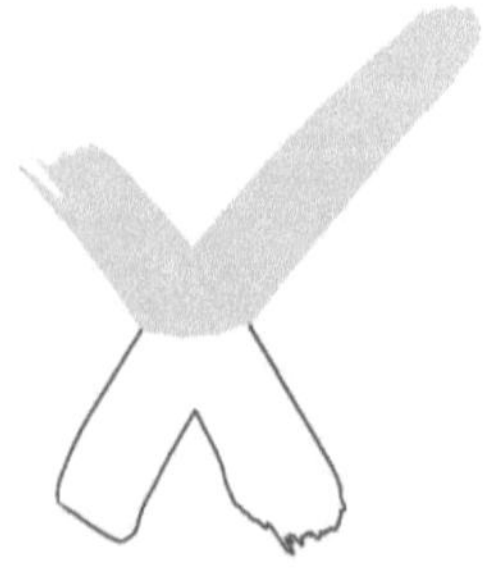

Failure is neither final nor fatal. Learning from failure creates a culture of resilience and growth.

Can you list 5 ways to stay calm when things are not going your way?

____

____

____

____

____

Staying calm allows you to manage your emotions, not feel overwhelmed, and respond to challenges in an effective way.

Do you find it difficult to stay optimistic during a setback? Can you think of 3 things you can do to stay optimistic?

____

____

____

____

____

Optimism helps you to reorient setbacks as temporary challenges and opportunities for growth rather than seeing them as dead ends.

Do you have a mentor or a role model you admire? Can you identify 3 things they do to handle adversity?

____

____

____

____

____

A mentor can play a key role in providing support and guidance to help you stay on track. Moreover, they can provide immense help in reevaluating your options and broadening your horizons with a unique perspective.

Have you tried using humour to lighten the moment when nothing is going your way? Can you think of the benefits of having a good sense of humour during adversity?

____

____

____

____

____

Adversity causes stress, but humour serves as an effective antidote to the stress hormone. At times, a lighter moment helps one distance oneself from the challenge and possibly come up with a different approach.

When was the last time you faced initial setbacks but kept at it? Can you identify what you did to remind yourself of your purpose and stay on track?

____

____

____

____

____

Aligning with your 'why' and purpose helps you stay motivated even during adversity.

Can you identify a challenge that you overcame in spite of initial setbacks? Which of your strengths did you leverage? How can you ensure that you always adopt a strength-focused approach during a crisis?

____

____

____

____

Leveraging strengths increases your probability of success and helps you stay confident in spite of initial setbacks.

INSTILLING OWNERSHIP

President Kennedy was visiting the NASA Space Centre in 1962, but he lost his way in the building. He bumped into a janitor in the service corridor and introduced himself, hoping the gentleman could help him find the way.

"Hi, I'm Jack Kennedy. What are you doing here?" The janitor replied, "Sir, I'm helping put a man on the moon."

The janitor wouldn't have been incorrect if he had mentioned that he cleaned the floors or maintained the hygiene of the area. But he went beyond his job description and identified with the larger vision. He felt he was playing an active role and wasn't a mere bystander!

This is a terrific story of ownership. The purpose of the mission was not lost or watered down as one cascaded to the base level of the pyramid.

Unfortunately, I went down quite a few rabbit holes to validate this story. There is no specific reference to this anecdote, and it might just be another urban legend. But it doesn't take away anything from what the gold standard of ownership should look like.

In fact, in the modern workplace, ownership is best demonstrated by the founding teams of most startups. Not everyone will wear a co-founder's badge. Most won't be fortunate enough to have stock ownership. But that doesn't come in the way of demonstrating the form of ownership that really matters.

If you pore over the LinkedIn profiles of most founding team members of a startup, from CEO to intern, the headline will read, 'Building XYZ'. This is another fabulous example of taking ownership.

As per the 2024 State of the Global Workplace report by Gallup, a mere 23% of employees feel engaged at work. Common sense tells us that with these dismal levels of engagement, the ownership score can't be dramatically higher either. Unfortunately, 'freaky Friday' celebrations and team-building activities don't necessarily move the needle with respect to ownership.

Of late, many established corporations have added 'founder's mindset' and 'entrepreneurial' as key values and competencies. This is the easy part. The challenge lies in instilling it in every team member.

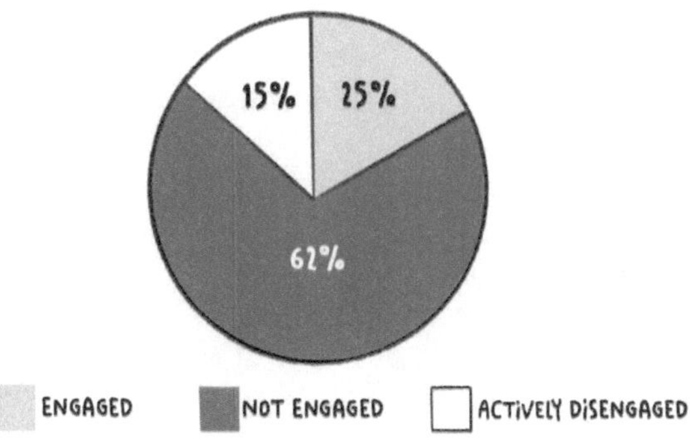

How do you get every team member to shed the 'not my circus, not my monkeys' attitude and become proactive, self-motivated, and take ownership?

After all, ownership is not an outcome – it is a mindset.

Scan the QR code to unlock the best practices to build the ownership mindset.

How comfortable are you in taking responsibility for failure? Can you identify 3 things you can do to demonstrate ownership even if the outcome is not favourable?

____

____

____

____

____

Taking responsibility is the first step in moving from the victim's seat to the driver's seat.

When was the last time you volunteered to lead a project? Can you identify a few things you can do to enhance your ownership quotient further?

____

____

____

____

____

Overcoming the fear and uncertainty of trying something new propels us beyond our comfort zone and towards thriving.

Can you recollect the successful completion of a task or a project for which you were responsible? How did it feel? Can you identify 3 things you did that ensured success?

____

____

____

____

Reflecting on past achievements helps us evaluate what worked and increases the probability of repeating the success formula in future tasks and projects.

Think of the most important project you are working on. Can you identify 3 things you can do to ensure all your peers and team members are working towards a shared vision?

____

____

____

____

Working towards a shared vision or purpose fosters greater clarity, aligns efforts, and enhances a sense of ownership and responsibility.

When was the last time you were not able to keep a commitment, like when you missed a deadline? How did it make you feel? Can you identify 3 things you can do to reduce lapses, if any?

____

____

____

____

Keeping commitments, however trivial, demonstrates a high degree of ownership and responsibility. In fact, it also inspires others to respond with increased ownership.

Do you tend to micromanage tasks? Can you identify 3 things you can do to empower your team members and peers to take more ownership?

____

____

____

____

____

Micromanagement is a potent ownership killer. It dampens the other person's motivation and intent as they get reduced to merely executing your ideas and plans.

Has the 'fear of failure' ever held you back from taking on a task or project? Can you identify 3 things you can do to overcome this fear in the future?

____

____

____

____

____

Fear of failure can hinder confidence and lead to shying away from demonstrating ownership and avoiding a challenging task or project.

Are you able to look at the big picture and understand how your contribution impacts the overall success? Can you identify 3 things you can do to always retain the wider perspective?

____

____

____

____

____

Being aware of the bigger picture and staying aligned with it helps you stay motivated, demonstrate ownership, and take initiative.

When you delegate tasks, do you also delegate accountability? Can you think of a few ways in which you can dial up the responsibility, even for tasks that you delegate?

Always remember that only authority can be delegated, not accountability.

Can you recollect a project where you demonstrated a high degree of ownership and responsibility? How collaborative and inclusive were you during the execution? Can you identify 3 things you can do to increase collaboration without dialling down your ownership?

____

____

____

____

____

'My way or the highway' is not a sign of ownership! Being high on the ownership quotient doesn't entail completing all your tasks by yourself but harnessing the collective strength and wisdom of the group.

WORKING TOGETHER

Whether you are a die-hard fan of the Marvel Cinematic Universe or just a casual viewer – I can bet you had goosebumps when a battered Captain America screams out the war cry during the climax of Avengers Endgame.

From individual superheroes flying solo to becoming part of a dream team, even fantasy movies now incorporate a strong reality check when it comes to the power of collaboration.

In the world of sports, teams that excel on a continuous basis don't rely on a few superstars but the collective might and grit of all the players. And while the scoreboard won't capture every small contribution, the final scoreline is usually a good indicator of the collaborative spirit.

Most of us are aware of the Olympics motto—*Citius, Altius, Fortius*—which is Latin for 'Faster, Higher, Stronger.' Pierre de Coubertin proposed this motto in 1924, stating,

"These 3 words represent a programme of moral beauty." This motto stood the test of time for almost 100 years before a new word was included right before the Tokyo Olympics in 2021.

The new word was 'communiter.' It means 'together'.

Citius, Altius, Fortius, Communiter

After all, the whole is always larger than the sum of its parts. This compounding phenomenon is probably the magic formula for collaboration.

Yet, our workplace still needs to master the collaboration code.

As per research by Salesforce – A whopping 86% of employees cite lack of collaboration as the primary reason for workplace failure. Ironically, most leading organisations would have posters in conference rooms and at receptions spotlighting collaboration as a core value. This gap needs addressing, and the need is immediate!

In fact, this gap seems to have been accentuated with the rise in remote working. Distance is often blamed for being a collaboration killer. I am sure it is not easy to collaborate across teams and time zones. But, always remember - Collaboration is seldom about proximity, skills, and tools. It is always about will and intent.

Here are a few popular myths with respect to collaboration in the workplace:

- Collaboration implies consensus and compromise.
- Collaboration is time-consuming.
- Diverse teams can't collaborate.
- Remote working kills collaboration.

You might want to take a few seconds to reflect on whether you have been feeding any of these myths and how you can snap out of it!

Henry Ford rightly said, "Coming together is a beginning, staying together is progress, and working together is a success."

Scan the QR code to unlock the best practices to master collaboration at the workplace.

Do you prefer working with people who are similar to you or with a diverse group? Can you identify a few things you can do to ensure diversity in every group you work with?

____

____

____

____

____

A diverse group of people have different perspectives and strengths, resulting in superior outcomes.

Are you allergic to conflicts? Do you prefer to avoid conflict or confront it? Can you identify 3 things you can do to handle conflicts effectively while working with a diverse group?

____

____

____

____

____

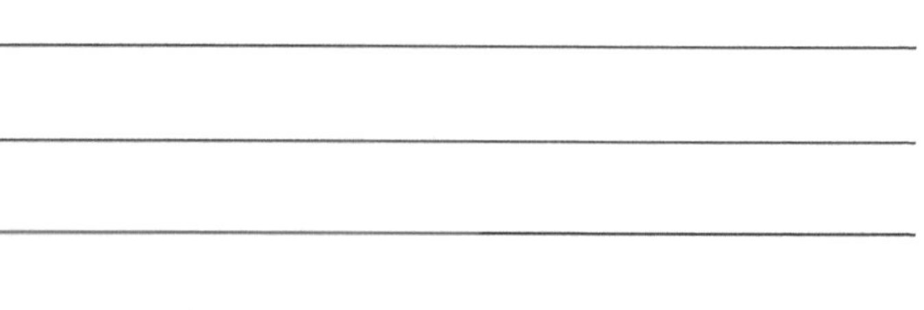

Effective conflict resolution strategies help prevent misunderstandings from escalating into larger issues and derailing a collaborative effort.

Can you articulate your team's 'Why' or the common purpose that all of you are working towards? What can you do to ensure everyone is on the same page?

____

____

____

____

____

Common purpose is probably the single biggest determinant of successful collaboration.

Can you identify the collaboration tools you use to improve productivity? Can you think of 3 more such tools or platforms that you can explore in the next 2 weeks?

____

____

____

____

____

Leveraging technology can help your team collaborate better and improve productivity and innovation.

Which was the last team win that all of you celebrated together? How did that feel? Can you identify 3 benefits of collectively celebrating wins, however small?

____

____

____

____

____

Celebrating wins, no matter how small, helps team members recognise each other's efforts and builds trust.

What are your team's top 3 values? Has this been articulated or left to assumption? Can you identify 3 things that will ensure everyone has a buy-in on the shared values?

____

____

____

____

____

While the strengths and perspectives of everyone in the team might differ, it is important to inculcate shared values to increase cooperation and reduce conflict.

How open are you to receiving feedback? Similarly, how effective is your style of giving feedback? Can you identify 3 things you can do to ensure your feedback is unbiased and effective?

____

____

____

____

Continuous and constructive feedback strengthens trust and builds a performance-focused team.

Every team comprises a few introverts who are hesitant to participate and contribute ideas. What are the few things you can do to encourage them to speak up?

____

____

____

____

____

Encouraging active participation from everyone helps build engagement and enhances collaboration.

If you asked everyone in the team to articulate the goal, would they give the same answer? What are the 3 things you can do to establish clear goals before commencing a project?

____

____

____

____

____

Establishing clear goals and expectations ensures everyone is marching to the same beat and in the same direction.

At times, does your ego get in the way of collaborating? Can you identify 3 things you can do to keep your ego tucked away while working with others?

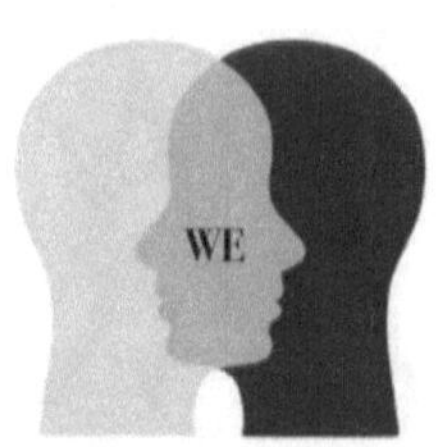

Ego is the enemy of collaboration. It is as simple as that.

REGULATING EMOTIONS

*"If you can meet with Triumph and Disaster,
And treat those 2 impostors just the same."*

These iconic lines from Rudyard Kipling's *If* greet you at the entrance to the Centre Court at Wimbledon.

But how can this be true? Athletes tend to wear their emotions on their sleeves, which is often mistaken for passion and drive.

Let's go back to the finals of the inaugural IPL in 2008. Two worthy teams were in a face-off: Chennai Super Kings, led by India's most popular cricketer, MS Dhoni, and the underdogs, Rajasthan Royals, led by the iconic Shane Warne.

Batting first, CSK scored a modest 163 runs. In response, the Royals were struggling at 42 for the loss of 3 wickets. At the halfway stage, Rajasthan's 2 most successful batters were at the crease, but neither of them was able to accelerate. Dhoni introduced Chennai's best bowler – Muralitharan.

And the strategy worked! On the 3rd ball of the over, the dangerous Yusuf Pathan tried to break the shackles and smash the ball out of the park. Instead, he skied it with Chennai's safest fielder, Suresh Raina, positioned under the ball. Unfortunately, Raina fumbled, and the ball popped out of his hands. In Murali's next over, Pathan smoked him for 2 consecutive sixes. He hit another 2 sixes a few overs later and sealed Chennai's fate.

Raina didn't just drop the catch but also the championship! Most captains would be livid, but not Dhoni.

Just after losing the match, he got his team in a huddle, laughed and joked with them. Even when Dhoni was asked if the missed catch was a turning point, he laughed it off and said, "We lost as a team. There were a few errors in batting and bowling. We're not really unhappy or bogged down by it. We'll go back to our hotel and enjoy it. That's what sport is all about."

MS Dhoni is a legend and fittingly called 'Captain Cool'. He is the only captain to win the T20 World Cup, 50-over World Cup and the Champions Trophy. He was also the captain of the team that faced a humiliating 4-0 drubbing in a test series in England and Australia, respectively, in 2011. His expression or demeanour didn't change after winning or losing. He truly embodies Kipling's words.

All of us have 2 versions of ourselves residing inside us. Depending on the situation, we can unleash the *'rage'* version or calmly present the *'sage'* version. Over time, our choice becomes a byproduct of our reflex action.

Suppose you have an important presentation to deliver to the senior leadership team. This is your moment to shine. But as luck would have it, your laptop refuses to boot, and you are unable to access the backup copy. The trainee who was tasked with the full tech check didn't show up. How will you react?

Will we meet your 'rage' or 'sage' version? If this were a game of snakes and ladders, a perfect presentation might have presented you with a ladder of opportunity. An emotional meltdown, however, would be a tragic slide down a slippery slope.

While the outcome of the board game depends solely on the roll of the dice, what happens in the boardroom is a controllable act if you want it to be.

Emotional regulation is the simple act where you control your emotions—not the other way around.

Scan the QR code to unlock the best practices to master emotional regulation.

Recall an incident when you got really angry at work. Did you have to face the consequences of that outburst? Identify 3 things you can do to control your anger.

____

____

____

____

____

Strony emotions switch off the thinking function of our brain. Identifying our feelings and reflecting on them calms us down.

Identify a recurring fear that hampers your progress. What does it feel like? Can you identify the trigger and how you can tackle the fear for good?

____

____

____

____

____

FEAR is False Evidence Appearing Real! Often, analysing it in a calm and rational way is all it takes to free ourselves from it.

When was the last time you showed empathy toward a colleague or a friend? How did it make you feel? Can you identify 3 benefits of demonstrating empathy?

____

____

____

____

____

Empathy eliminates judgement, helps demonstrate compassion, and builds deep connections.

When was the last time you felt emotionally vulnerable due to a challenge at work? Can you identify 3 things you can do to handle a similar situation next time?

____

____

____

____

____

Challenges are better handled by stating facts and discussing them rather than through outbursts or repression.

Do you tend to bottle up your emotions during conflicts to avoid making things messier? Can you think of 3 reasons why bottling up is a bad strategy for resolving disagreements?

____

____

____

____

____

Bottling up emotions just buries the feeling instead of addressing them, turning them into a ticking time bomb.

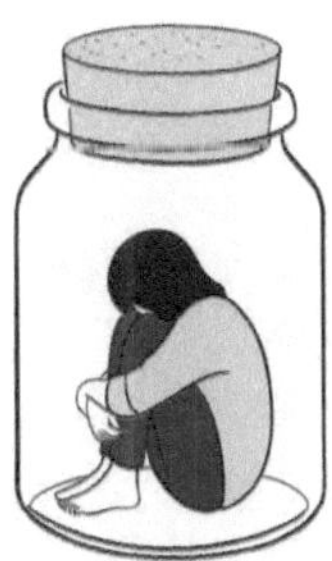

On a scale of 1 to 10 (with 1 being the hardest and 10 being the easiest), how easily can you say 'No'? Can you identify 3 things you can do to say 'no' the next time you lack the bandwidth to do something?

____

____

____

____

____

Setting healthy boundaries is essential for emotional well-being. Knowing when to say 'no' helps maintain a balanced workload and preserves energy.

Have you tried taking a 5-second pause to reflect before unleashing the fury of your emotions? Can you think of 3 benefits of a 'pause and reflect' strategy?

____

____

____

____

____

Taking a moment to pause and reflect can be incredibly valuable, especially in high-pressure situations. This simple act can prevent knee-jerk reactions.

It is natural to feel resentment towards people you think are luckier or have unfairly achieved more than they deserve. Can you identify 3 things you can do to dial down the resentment and eventually eliminate it?

____

____

____

____

____

"Feeling resentment is like consuming poison and expecting the other person to die." It does more harm to you than you can imagine.

When was the last time you felt envy and jealousy toward someone else? Can you identify 3 negative effects of being jealous?

____

____

____

____

The simple truth is that we cannot have it all. If we allow jealousy into our hearts and minds, we must say goodbye to peace and happiness.

Do you control your emotions, or do your emotions control you? Can you think of a few instances in the last 2 weeks when your emotions influenced your actions?

____

____

____

____

____

Regularly reflecting on emotional experiences can lead to personal growth, offering insights that help you manage future situations more effectively.

STAYING ON TRACK

We have all grown up obsessing over ambitious goals. Author James Clear makes a compelling case for systems in his bestseller *Atomic Habits*. He argues, "Winners and losers have the same goals, but the systems used to achieve those goals are what differentiate them."

In the late 1800s, the Romans had devised a rather barbaric way to keep their advancing troops on track. Whenever the army crossed a river to invade a new territory, the commander-general would order the bridges to be burned, thus preventing the troops from retreating. In fact, this drastic act is the origin of the phrase 'Don't burn your bridges.'

Let us look at a more inspiring example. In 1978, James started with the idea of creating bagless vacuum cleaners that didn't lose suction. He spent the next 15 years creating 5,127 different prototypes. He said, "By 2,627, my wife and I were really counting our pennies. By 3,727, my wife was giving art lessons for some extra cash."

In spite of multiple failed attempts, the vacuum cleaner prototype kept losing suction, but James didn't lose hope. He stayed the course, and within 5 years, his patent was creating waves. His brand became one of the fastest-growing vacuum cleaners in the world. In fact, James didn't stop with vacuum cleaners; his approach to doubling down on R&D and creating patents expanded the company's product portfolio into hair dryers, air purifiers, fans, and robot vacuums.

The man with 5,127 prototypes is none other than Sir James Dyson, and his innovative company is none other than Dyson Ltd. Even today, the company makes a 6-times higher investment in R&D than competitors. In fact, all Dyson products sell at a significant premium. For example, the upright vacuum cleaner by them sells at an almost 20x premium over the cheapest alternative.

We are encouraged to dream big! The more audacious the goal, the greater the cheer and support. But setting sights on an ambitious goal is only the beginning. That's when the real journey begins. And the only winning formula to stay on track over the long haul is to be process-focused, not result-focused—just like Sir James Dyson.

Let's look at the anatomy of a goal. Irrespective of the impact and scale of the goal, it largely comprises:

- **Purpose:** This provides direction and meaning, like the North Star.
- **Process:** This is the system and a collection of time-bound activities that will help achieve the objective.
- **Passion:** The positive energy that keeps us going.
- **Perseverance:** The superpower to stay determined in spite of setbacks.

Consider any critical goal in your life and do a quick status check to see if all the Ps are covered. Here is a quick snapshot of the impact in case any one of the P is missing:

PURPOSE	PROCESS	PASSION	PERSEVERANCE	OUTCOME
✗	✓	✓	✓	DEMOTIVATED
✓	✗	✓	✓	UNSUSTAINABLE & INEFFICIENT
✓	✓	✗	✓	NON STARTER
✓	✓	✓	✗	GIVE UP!

If we go back to the example of Sir James Dyson, you will realise his journey of building the best vacuum cleaner had all the Ps covered.

- Purpose: **Check.**
- Process: **Check.**
- Passion: **Check.**
- Perseverance: **Check.**

The next time you are taking on an audacious goal, always remember to align your purpose, design your process, crank up your passion, and build your perseverance. It is the easiest way to stay on track.

Scan the QR code to unlock the best practices to stay on track.

What is the most important challenge you want to overcome? Can you try to break the larger goal into 5 smaller, more manageable goals?

____

____

____

____

____

If we set smaller goals for ourselves that are reasonable, challenging, yet achievable, we don't feel overwhelmed by the larger challenge.

Have you been trying to solve a problem for a while? Can you identify 3 benefits of taking a break and returning to it after a few days?

____

____

____

____

____

Taking a break is not a sign of weakness but rather a strategic move towards enhanced problem-solving and increased creativity.

On a scale of 1 to 10, rate your perseverance quotient. Can you identify 3 things you can do to improve your perseverance and stay on track despite initial setbacks?

____

____

____

____

____

Perseverance helps you build resilience, stay motivated, and remain focused, even if things don't go your way.

Consider a critical goal that you want to achieve. Can you articulate your true purpose and why the goal is important?

____

____

____

____

____

Having a strong purpose and being aligned with it increases your optimism and confidence to take on a goal, no matter how challenging.

How can you become 'indistractible'? Identify 5 activities that waste your time and easily distract you? How can you avoid them?

____

____

____

____

____

By eliminating distractions, you can dedicate your full attention to the problem that needs to be solved.

Think of the last problem that you solved successfully. Can you identify a few things that you had done that contributed to the success?

____

____

____

____

____

Revisiting past successes can provide insights and inspire confidence to overcome a current challenge.

Can you identify 3 of your key strengths that will help you stay on track towards achieving a critical goal?

____

____

____

____

____

Contrary to conventional wisdom, focusing on your strengths (rather than solely improving your weaknesses) can increase the probability of success.

Could you be making some assumptions while evaluating your current challenge? Can you identify 3 assumptions and question their validity?

____

____

____

____

____

Assumptions limit our thinking and prevent us from considering alternative solutions.

If a friend was facing the same challenge as you – what 5 things would you advise them to do? What is stopping you from imbibing them yourself?

____

____

____

____

____

When you are giving advice to others, you have the clarity of distance, making it easier to think of effective solutions because you're not consumed by the challenge.

Do you feel stuck or tempted to give up any goal that you are pursuing? Can you identify 5 people (mentors, manager, friends, etc) you can reach out to for a fresh perspective?

____

____

____

____

____

Seeking different perspectives can help you see things from different angles, learn new information, and challenge your existing beliefs.

FINDING JOY

Let's begin this chapter by playing a simple game called Happ-a-Minute!

In 60 seconds, can you list everything that makes you happy? The extent of delight is insignificant, if it makes you joyful, add it to the list. Your time starts now.

Hopefully, you have managed to identify at least 8 to 10 'top of the mind' activities that make you happy. Now, revisit your list and answer these questions:

Beyond the first few, did you find it tough to identify things that make you happy?

How many activities on the list would require a lot of effort and money to implement?

How many of these activities have you done in the last 2 weeks?

If you have done most of the activities from your list in the past 2 weeks, you deserve a pat on the back!

From teaching an elective on happiness to young MBA graduates to facilitating happiness workshops for senior leaders, I always begin with this exercise. And the last question invariably cuts too close to the bone.

In a flash, I see the look of 'Aha!' when the penny

drops. While most of us spend a lifetime blaming others for the cause of our unhappiness, we continue to be the chief culprit. After all, happiness is an inside job.

Here's an interesting anecdote (or perhaps just an urban legend): A young schoolboy in Liverpool was asked what he wanted to be when he grew up. He said, "Happy!"

His teacher bluntly told him that he didn't understand the assignment, to which the boy aptly retorted: "You don't understand life."

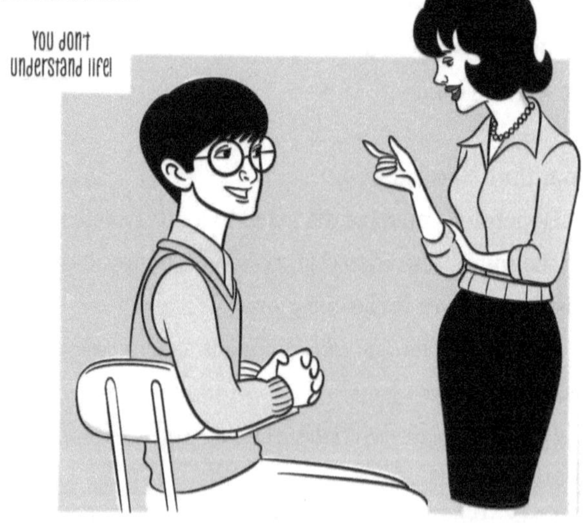

That young boy with such profound words of wisdom was John Lennon, the songwriter and lead singer of one of the greatest music bands, The Beatles!

So, how can you be happy? There might be no 'one-size-fits-all' answer to this million-dollar question. Let's borrow a few principles from neuroscience to try and answer the question.

The 4 neurochemicals that are responsible for happiness are Dopamine, Oxytocin, Serotonin, and Endorphin. They aptly combine to form the acronym – **DOSE.**

⊙ *Dopamine* is released in response to what the brain perceives as pleasurable or beneficial. From extra likes on an Instagram post to indulging in a calorie-loaded chocolate cake, the dopamine surge is what we all crave! Dopamine also helps us work towards goals and provides a surge of pleasure in accomplishing them. More than achieving the goal, it is the anticipation that triggers dopamine. It is not just about the pursuit of happiness but also the happiness of pursuit.

⊙ *Oxytocin* is often referred to as the 'cuddle' hormone and is released when you connect with people. It creates intimacy and trust while developing strong relationships. It creates a feeling of empathy, which in turn helps us bond with others.

⊙ *Serotonin* is triggered when we engage in social good, such as acts of kindness, generosity, or feeling gratitude. It flows when you feel significant. It plays the role of a mood regulator.

⊙ *Endorphin* production is stimulated by exercise. Don't you feel a sense of euphoria after a good workout or playing a sport? This is often referred to as the 'Runner's High'. Endorphins are 3 times as powerful as morphine without the side effects. They, therefore, subside physical stress or fatigue and leave you focusing on the happy feeling.

It might be a good idea to circle back to your happy

list and evaluate if your activities cover the DOSE spectrum.

In fact, understanding the chemicals of happiness is a logical way to comprehend whether you need money to be happy. Besides the transient dopamine spikes, you don't really need to be rich to be happy. But happiness is certainly the new rich!

Scan the QR code to learn the results of Harvard's 75-year research on what makes a person truly happy.

Can you identify 3 things you did in the last week that truly made you happy? Make a note of them and reflect how can you repeat these activities more often.

____

____

____

____

____

Journaling your happy moments actively increases your happiness by sharpening your focus and enhancing mindfulness.

Do you enjoy regular exercise? Can you identify 3 things you can do to become more regular with your workouts?

____

____

____

____

____

Regular exercise releases endorphins, a neurochemical responsible for happiness.

Can you identify 3 things you can do together with your family every week?

____

____

____

____

____

Oxytocin, a neurochemical of happiness, is released when you spend time with your loved ones.

Can you recollect a time when someone was kind to you when you least expected it? How did it make you feel? Can you identify 3 random acts of kindness that you can do?

____

____

____

____

A random act of kindness triggers serotonin, a neurochemical linked to happiness.

What is the one thing that makes you leap out of bed every morning with joy and excitement?

____

____

____

____

____

When your skills align with your passion and purpose, and you get paid for it, you reach the pinnacle of joy and find your 'Ikigai.'

Can you identify a hobby that brings you joy? How much time do you spend on it each week? And can you think of 3 ways to carve out more time for it?

____

____

____

____

____

Pursuing a hobby relaxes your mind, enhances your mood, and makes you happier.

Can you identify 3 people you are grateful to and write a short thank you note to them?

____

____

____

____

____

Gratitude is often viewed as the meta-strategy of happiness, as it fosters connection and a sense of being blessed.

Can you list down 5 things that bring you joy that don't cost a lot of money and are effortless?

____

____

____

____

____

Studies reveal that happiness is found in experiences rather than material possessions

What success do you wish for that will make you truly happy? Does happiness always have to be linked to success?

____

____

____

____

Contrary to popular belief, the *Global Meta Survey of Happiness Research* reveals that happiness is the precursor to success, not merely its outcome.

Is there a social cause you are deeply passionate about? Can you identify 3 things that you can do to make a meaningful contribution?

____

____

____

____

____

Philanthropy releases serotonin, the neurochemical that boosts happiness for the giver, the receiver, and those who witness it.

MASTERING THE UNSTUCK FORMULA

Imagine a person is stuck in quicksand. It is a daunting feeling of being helpless and immobile. The harder they try, the deeper they sink.

Life's challenges can be quite similar. You feel overwhelmed, and it seems like your hands are tied in a knot. And the more vehemently you try to free yourself, the knot just seems to get tighter. All you wish for is a little wiggle room. But you are terribly stuck, and there seems to be no way out!

If it were the movies, someone would make a heroic entry and save the day. But you are the 'hero' of your life, and you need to crack the 'unstuck' code for yourself.

So here it is— a simple framework that's not a lifeboat to rescue you from drowning but rather a 'lighthouse' to illuminate the path that you can pursue.

True to the ethos of this book, the framework is fittingly called REFLECT. It is the backronym (yes, that is a word!) for:

- **RE**ality
- **FL**ip
- **E**xplore options
- **C**ommit
- **T**rack

Let's dive deep into each step:

REality

Kickstart your 'Reflection' process by identifying the challenge in a short, succinct sentence. We are often tempted to focus on the 'drama' and go round and round in circles. Try answering the question: *What challenges are you currently facing?*

Reflecting on this question helps to calm down the 'Feeler' and activate the 'Thinker'. Are you ready to put on your thinking cap?

A few questions you can ask yourself:

- Can you summarise your feelings in one line?
- On a scale of 1–10, how important is it for you to solve this challenge? (Ideally, if it is not a 7+, it might not be a real challenge)
- What areas of your work/life does this challenge impact?

Flip

In this stage, you take the first step on the bridge that takes you from being stuck to becoming unstuck. As the name suggests, you flip the situation from what it is and visualise what you want it to be - your best-case scenario.

The objective of 'flip' is to dial down the problem focus and rev up the solution-focus.

A few questions you can ask yourself:

- *What would an ideal situation look like?*
- *How does the best-case scenario feel?*
- *If a newspaper were to profile your inspirational journey, what would the headline read? (This is one of my favourite questions, and you can tweak it to the title of your memoir or a movie poster)*

Exploring Options

Now, it's time to put on your explorer's hat and switch on your GPS! You need to identify all the options that will help you stay on course and reach your destination. There are multiple ways in which you can travel from point A to point B.

At this stage, you simply need to identify all the options. Here is a pro tip: Pick quantity over quality.

A few questions you can ask yourself:

- *Can you identify a few options that will help you reach your ideal situation?*
- *Can you think of a few more?*
- *If a friend faced a similar challenge, what advice would you give them?*
- *Can you identify a few of the strengths you can leverage to get unstuck?*

Commit

If the exploration phase was about creating a wide funnel to identify a large number of options, the commit phase is where you use a tight filter to narrow it down to a limited choice that will work for you.

It is imperative to commit to a plan that you will find easier to adhere to (not what others suggest or what social media influencers propound). When you commit to select action points, it is akin to signing a mental contract with yourself and building accountability.

A few questions you can ask yourself:

- *On a scale of 1–10, how committed are you to staying the course for each option? (Rate every option and consider the ones that score 8+).*
- *Identify the options that will help you achieve your goal in the most sustained and comfortable manner.*
- *Shortlist the options with which you would like to begin your journey?*

Track

Peter Drucker is credited with the quote: "What gets measured, gets managed."

My favourite example is the '1 in 60' rule in aviation. A mere 1 degree of error by an aircraft results in a 1 kilometre deviation for every 60 kilometres travelled. What this means is that if you are flying from Chennai to New Delhi, a 1-degree error by the pilot will make you miss the swanky airport in New Delhi and land on the Delhi-Jaipur highway in Manesar.

Just having an action plan that you are committed to is not enough. A regular status check will help you course-correct and stay on track.

A few questions you can ask yourself:

- *How frequently do you wish to track progress for each action point? (Daily, Weekly, or Fortnightly)*
- *Do you want to have a goal buddy who can help you stay on track?*
- *(After a few weeks) — Are there a few action plans that you want to add, remove, or tweak?*

This framework can help you get unstuck across personal and professional challenges. From unlocking the next phase of growth in your career or getting fitter, this is a simple tool to get unstuck with a plan that is customised for you.

Always remember:

The more you 'REFLECT'

The more you become!